# Viking Life

# INVASION AND SETTLEMENT

## Nicola Barber

First published in 2010 by Wayland

Copyright © Wayland 2010

Wayland
338 Euston Road
London NW1 3BH

Wayland Australia
Level 17/207 Kent Street
Sydney NSW 2000

Series Editor: Nicola Edwards
Series Consultant: Annette Trolle
Designer: Jane Hawkins
Picture Researcher: Kathy Lockley

British Library Cataloguing in Publication Data
Barber, Nicola.
  Viking life.
  Invasion and settlement.
  1. Vikings--Foreign countries--Juvenile literature.
  2. Cities and towns, Viking--Juvenile literature.
  I. Title
  909'.04395-dc22

ISBN 978 0 7502 6385 6

Picture acknowledgements
Aahus Kunstmuseum/Arhus Denmark/Gianni Dagli Orti/The Art Archive: 12, 29;
The Art Gallery Collection/Alamy: 13; Anthony Baggett/iStockphoto: 21;
Timothy Ball/iStockphoto: 14; Andrew Barker/iStockphoto: Cover (main), 8;
Stefano Bianchetti/Corbis: Title page, 18; Peter V. Bianchi/NationalGeographic/
Getty: 24;British Library, London, UK (Harl 2278f98v)/BridgemanArt Library,
London: 27; Werner Forman Archive/National Museum of Denmark, Copenhagen: 5, 11;
Werner Forman Archive/Statens Historiska Museum,Stockholm: 16; Les Gibbon/Alamy: 7;
GM Photo Images/Alamy: 22; Historiska Museet Stockholm/Gianni Dagli Orti/The Art Archive: 26; Ian
Thompson: 6; INTERFOTO/Alamy: Cover (inset), 4, 20, 23; Kharbine-Tapabor/Collection J. Vigne/The Art
Archive: 19; Gareth McCormack/Alamy: 10;Nationalmuseet/National Museum of Denmark, Copenhagen: 9;
Courtesy The Rooms Corporation of Newfoundland and Labrador, Canada  Provincial Museum Division:
25, 28; Professor Mark A. Wilson: 17;© York Archaeological Trust: 15

The author and publisher would like to thank Torkild Waagaard for his kind permission
to reproduce his artwork of a Viking helmet on the panels in this book.

Printed in China

Wayland is a division of Hachette Children's Books, an Hachette UK company.

www.hachette.co.uk

# Contents

Words in **bold** can be found in the glossary.

# The Viking world

The Vikings came from Scandinavia, the region of northern Europe that is made up of modern-day Denmark, Norway and Sweden. From the 8th to the 11th centuries, many Vikings left their homelands on journeys of piracy, discovery and **commerce**. This time is often called the 'Viking Age'.

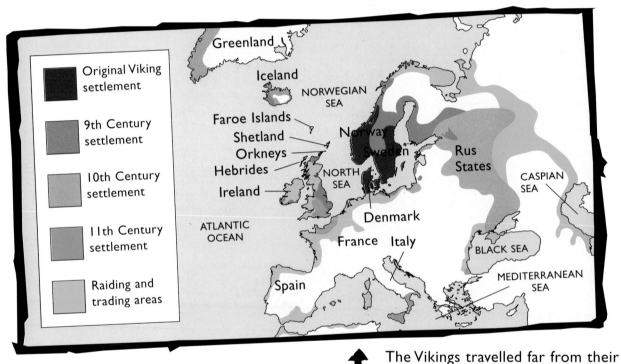

| | |
|---|---|
| ■ | Original Viking settlement |
| ■ | 9th Century settlement |
| ■ | 10th Century settlement |
| ■ | 11th Century settlement |
| ■ | Raiding and trading areas |

Greenland
Iceland
NORWEGIAN SEA
Faroe Islands
Shetland
Orkneys
Hebrides
Ireland
NORTH SEA
Norway
Sweden
Rus States
CASPIAN SEA
ATLANTIC OCEAN
Denmark
France  Italy
BLACK SEA
MEDITERRANEAN SEA
Spain

⬆ The Vikings travelled far from their Scandinavian homelands, journeying across seas and along rivers.

## Who were the Vikings?

The word Viking comes from the **Old Norse** language, meaning 'pirate', or 'piracy'. Not all Vikings were pirates or **raiders**. The people of Scandinavia were farmers and fishers, and while many Vikings set out on exciting voyages, many others remained on their farms in their homeland. Vikings from different parts of Scandinavia travelled in different directions. Those from Norway set out westwards on voyages across the North Sea. The Danish Vikings also sailed west. Meanwhile, the Swedish Vikings travelled eastwards, where they were known by the local people as the 'Rus'.

# What did they do?

The Vikings were superb sailors. They used their skills to sail across seas and along rivers, raiding and **plundering** as they went. From the earliest raids in the 8th century, the sight of Viking ships on the horizon was enough to spark fear and panic in communities across Europe. The Vikings attacked places in the British Isles, France and even as far south as Spain and Africa. They were also traders, explorers and **colonizers**, sailing west to Iceland, Greenland and even as far as North America.

⬆ The remains of a Viking settlement on the Brough of Birsay, a tiny island off the Orkney Islands. This was one of the places settled by the Vikings in the 800s.

## Written at the time

An Irish monk wrote these words in the margin of a book on a night when the weather outside was so bad he could be confident there would be no Viking raids:

'The wind is fierce tonight
It tosses the sea's white hair
I fear no wild Vikings
Sailing the quiet main [ocean].'

# Monastery raids

In the 790s the Vikings began to raid and plunder the **monasteries** of northern England and Scotland. The monasteries were full of riches – and they were unprotected.

## The first raids

Warning of what was to come was given in 789, when three Viking ships arrived off the coast of southern England. A local official was sent to greet the ships – but the Vikings killed him. In 793, the first recorded Viking raid took place on the monastery of Lindisfarne. The monastery stood on a small island (Holy Island) off the coast of northeast England. The island's long, sandy beach was the perfect landing place for the Viking **longships**. The Vikings plundered the monastery of its wealth and killed many of its monks. Then they left. The raid was clearly successful, as the following year more Viking ships arrived to attack monasteries further south at Jarrow and Wearmouth.

↑ Today, Holy Island is home to the dramatic hilltop castle seen here. The monastery that was attacked by the Vikings has long since disappeared.

# Written at the time

This description of a Viking raid on a monastery in Wearmouth in 794 is taken from the *Anglo-Saxon Chronicle*:

'... the heathen armies [the Vikings] spread devastation among the Northumbrians, and plundered the monastery of King Everth at the mouth of the Wear. There, however, some of their leaders were slain; and some of their ships also were shattered to pieces by the violence of the weather; many of the crew were drowned; and some, who escaped alive to the shore, were soon dispatched [killed] at the mouth of the river.'

## Terrifying and shocking

The Viking raids were unexpected and terrifying. They were also shocking because they attacked Christian holy places. English writers of the time called the Vikings '**pagans**' and '**heathens**'. In 795, the Vikings raided another holy site – the monastery of St Columba on the island of Iona off the west coast of Scotland. Once again, the Viking raiders were attracted by the wealth of the monastery. Their attacks caused outrage in the Christian world.

⬆ This precious wooden casket, covered with brass decorations, is an example of the kind of treasure the Vikings seized during their raids on monasteries.

# Viking attacks

From the beginning of the Viking Age, Vikings from Norway established settlements in the Orkney and Shetland islands, and in the Hebrides off the northwest coast of Scotland. Meanwhile, Vikings from Denmark crossed the North Sea to attack the coast of England.

➡ The round tower at Turlough in County Mayo, Ireland. It was built some time between 900 and 1200. It is possible that towers such as this were built to protect communities and their treasures during Viking attacks.

## Into Ireland

The Norwegian Vikings used their island settlements as bases to travel even further afield. They invaded the Isle of Man, and then began to raid Ireland. At first these raids were 'hit-and-run' attacks – the Vikings used fast boats to come and go, and relied on surprising their victims. They Viking raiders grabbed whatever riches and goods they could, including **livestock**. They also took men and women to sell as slaves in their homelands. Sometimes, if the Vikings captured an important person, for example the head of a monastery, they would demand a **ransom** for his return.

Gradually the raids became bigger, more organised – and even more adventurous. The Vikings began to explore up rivers to raid settlements inland. They also built fortified bases, called *longphorts*, where they could spend the winters safely when the weather was too wild for sailing. One of these bases, established in 841, was on the River Liffey, on the east coast of Ireland. It was called Dubh-Linn (Black Pool) and it developed into a major Viking settlement. Today we know it as the capital of Ireland, Dublin.

## The Danes arrive

The Danish Vikings, meanwhile, were busy attacking the coast of England. In 850, a large fleet of ships landed in Kent, and Viking raiders stormed both Canterbury and London. At about the same time, Vikings from Denmark began to arrive in Ireland. They were not welcomed by the Norwegian Vikings, and there were many battles between the new arrivals and the Vikings from Norway.

➡ This is a ceremonial axe which would have belonged to an important Viking chieftan.

## A Viking Object

*This beautiful Viking axe was found in a burial mound at Mammen, Denmark. It is made from iron which has been finely decorated with silver. You can see the shape of a bird on the axe head. The Vikings used axes as effective weapons in battle.*

# Raids further afield

In 843, the Vikings plundered Nantes on the west coast of France. Then they established a winter base on the Isle de Noirmoutier, an island just off the French coast at the mouth of the Loire river.

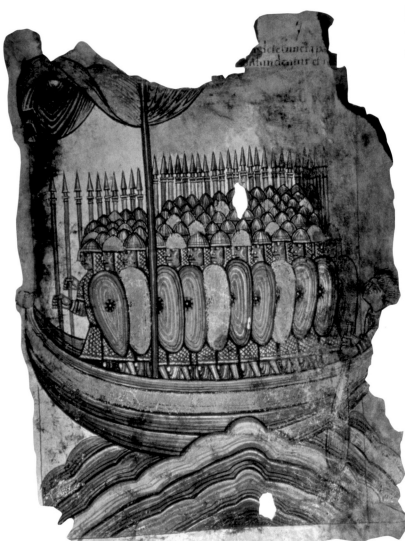

The Vikings arrive off the coast of Normandy, in northern France.

## Run away!

The monks who had lived at the abbey on Noirmoutier had already fled the island because of Viking raids in previous years, taking with them their most precious belongings for safekeeping. As Viking raids extended along the coast of France, people quickly learned to flee the attacks rather than stay and risk being killed or taken hostage.

## Up river

Just as in Ireland, the Vikings used rivers as an important means of travelling inland. Viking ships sailed up the Seine in the north, the Loire in the west and the Garonne in southern France, attacking towns far inland.

In 845 a Viking leader called Ragnar Lodbrok led an army of 5,000 warriors up the Seine to Paris. At that time Paris was part of the Frankish Empire. When the Vikings threatened to burn down the city, the king of the Franks, Charles the Bald, was forced to pay a fortune in ransom to make the Vikings go away.

## Into the Mediterranean

Some daring Vikings raided as far south as Spain and North Africa. The first recorded raid on Spain was in 844. In 859, a Viking fleet of about 62 ships set out from the Loire river on a long voyage of raiding that took it through the Strait of Gibraltar and as far as Italy. When the fleet returned in 862, it was only one-third of its original size, but the surviving ships carried immense riches back home with them.

A Viking fleet crosses the English Channel on its way to attack the French coast.

### Ragnar Lodbrok (Died c. 865)

*Ragnar Lodbrok was a famous Viking leader from Denmark, and a popular hero amongst the Vikings themselves. He was a raider and pirate, and was responsible for many attacks in France. He often demanded a ransom in return for leaving his victims alone – only to return later for more money. His luck ran out when he was shipwrecked off the English coast. One version of the story of his death tells that the local English king put Ragnar in a pit full of vipers (poisonous snakes), where he was bitten to death.*

# Settling Iceland

Not all Vikings were pirates and raiders. Some Vikings wanted to explore and settle new lands. In 815 a Viking called Floki of Rogaland set out from the Faroe Islands. He landed in a place he called *Ice-land*, which is the name we still know today.

## A new life

The Vikings saw that although Iceland had many volcanoes and **glaciers** inland, it also had a lot of good farming land along its coast. The sea was full of fish, at that time there were large forests, and there was **iron ore** in the ground for blacksmiths to make tools and weapons. Starting in the 870s, thousands of Viking families made the voyage across the North Sea from Norway and from Viking settlements in the north of England to start new lives on Iceland.

The Viking settlers organised themselves into small communities, each under the leadership of a **chieftain**. They built farmsteads with large halls where people lived, worked and slept. By 930, it is estimated that around 30,000 people were living in Iceland.

## The Althing

In 930, chieftains from across Iceland came together for the first time at a meeting of the Althing – the Icelandic general assembly. This meeting was held outdoors at Thingvellir, a place in western Iceland which was chosen because people from the most populated parts of the island could travel there easily. From 930, the Althing was held every year to proclaim the laws of the country. It also tried to settle disputes between rival chieftains – but there were still many quarrels that ended in violence.

Thingvellir in Iceland, where the Althing first met in 930. The site had good grazing, water and ample firewood for all the people who gathered there.

# Into Russia

While the Norwegian and Danish Vikings mostly looked west, the Swedish Vikings travelled east, deep into the European continent by river. They were known as the 'Rus' by the local people – and this is possibly the origin of the name 'Russia'.

## Viking traders

The Vikings who travelled east were not usually raiders and pirates. They were mostly merchants, who were keen to trade. We know about their travels from **archaeological** finds such as Viking weapons, graves and jewellery that have been uncovered all across European Russia.

Some of the main items traded by the Viking merchants were furs, **amber**, wax and honey. In return, they particularly prized silver coins, many of which came from the Islamic Empire. The Vikings took these Arab coins and melted them down into **ingots**, which were used to make silver jewellery.

↑ Silver coins such as these were in great demand by the Vikings.

# Long journeys

From the Baltic Sea the Vikings rowed their ships up rivers that took them far inland. They often had to take their boats out of the water and carry them around rapids. When they reached the end of these rivers, they hauled their ships overland to the upper reaches of other rivers such as the Dniepr and the Volga. The Dniepr took the Vikings to the Black Sea, from where they could reach the city of Constantinople, capital of the **Byzantine Empire**. The Volga led into the Caspian Sea, and to trade routes leading to Baghdad, at the heart of the **Islamic** world.

Many Vikings settled in places along the trade routes. Some of these settlements were trading places where Vikings mixed and lived with the local people. We know that Viking women lived in these settlements from graves that have been uncovered. Major trading centres included Kiev on the River Dnieper and Novgorod on the Volkhov river.

## A Viking Object

*When a Viking person died, he or she was often buried with all the objects needed for a life after death. These mounds next to the Volkhov river are possibly the burial places of powerful Viking chieftains who explored, traded and settled in Russia.*

⬆ Viking burial mounds on the Volkhov river, near Staraya Ladoga in present-day Russia. Staraya Ladoga was an important trading centre during the Viking Age.

# The siege of Paris

From around the 830s the Danish Vikings began to attack western Europe. Some of these attacks were raids, but others were organised campaigns with large, well-equipped armies.

## Viking army

In 885, the Danish Vikings sent a huge army up the River Seine. According to some sources there were 700 ships and 30,000 warriors, although we cannot know if these numbers are accurate. The Viking ships could not sail further than Paris because of two low bridges across the river – a wooden and a stone bridge on either side of the Ile de la Cité, an island in the middle of the Seine. The bridges had been built as fortifications, to prevent Viking raids further up the river.

## Paris attacked

The Vikings demanded a huge ransom, which was refused. The king of the Franks, Charles the Fat, was in Italy, so the defence of Paris was left to a local nobleman called Odo. The Vikings attacked Paris with arrows, catapults and fire.

The Vikings attack Paris in 885.

Odo and his 200 followers defended themselves by pouring hot wax and tar from the towers on the stone bridge.

## Siege

After a few weeks of furious battle, the Vikings dug in for a **siege**. They used crops and livestock from the surrounding countryside to feed their army. Meanwhile, the defenders inside the besieged city began to run out of food.

As **plague** and **famine** began to spread in the city, Odo managed to slip through the Viking lines. He went to Italy to plead with Charles the Fat for help.

The siege lasted for over a year before Charles the Fat arrived with a large army. The Vikings eventually withdrew, but only after receiving a large amount of silver in ransom.

➡

One of the Viking leaders to attack Paris was Rollo. He is shown here seizing a house in Normandy, France.

# Written at the time

The dramatic tale of the siege of Paris is described in The Annals of St Vaast:

'The Northmen [Vikings] ceased not to attack the city daily; many were killed and still more were disabled by wounds, and food began to give out in the city... Odo saw how the people were falling into despair, and he went forth secretly to seek aid from the nobles of the kingdom...'

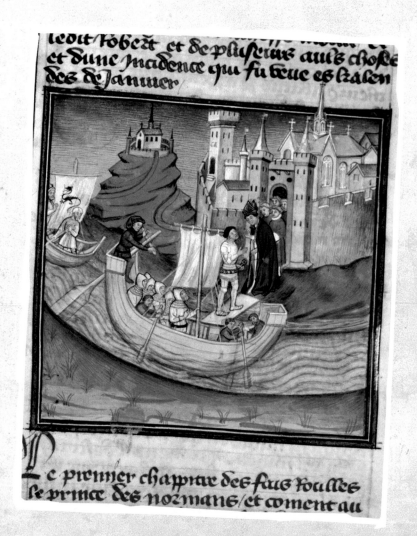

# The Vikings in England

In 865, the *Anglo-Saxon Chronicle* records that 'a great heathen army came into England and took up winter quarters in East Anglia…'. This largely Danish Viking army had several leaders, including the sons of Ragnar Lodbrok.

⬆ This image from the Bayeux Tapestry shows Viking longships at sea.

## The 'great army'

Over the next few years, the 'great army' marched up and down England. The Vikings captured York and conquered Northumbria. Then the Vikings returned to East Anglia. In 865 they had 'made peace' with the leaders of East Anglia – meaning probably that they took a large ransom from the East Angles. In 869, the Vikings fought the East Angles and killed their king, Edmund. After their victory over the East Angles the Vikings controlled most of eastern England from York south to London.

Next the Vikings turned their attention to the kingdom of Wessex, which lay in the southwest of England. Under the leadership of King Guthrum, the Vikings met forces led by King Alfred of Wessex near Reading. After much fighting, the two sides 'made peace' – once again the Vikings were paid to go away. The Viking armies then turned north into Mercia.

## King Alfred
## 849 CE – 899 CE

*King Alfred is often known as 'the Great' because of his success in fighting off Viking attacks during his reign. Although he was forced to 'make peace' with the Vikings several times, Alfred won a major victory against the Vikings in 878. After agreeing a treaty with Guthrum, Alfred set about reorganising the military defence of his kingdom. He built fortified towns, and set up a well-trained army and a small navy.*

## Settling down

After nearly ten years of moving around and fighting battles, the Viking leaders began to share out the land they had conquered. The earliest Viking settlements were in the 'land of the Northumbrians', but the Vikings also established themselves in Mercia and in East Anglia.

## Danelaw

Some time around 880 King Guthrum and King Alfred agreed a **treaty**. In it they agreed the boundaries between Alfred's kingdom of Wessex and a large area of eastern and northern England, known as the **Danelaw**, which came under Viking rule. After Alfred's death, however, his son (Edward) and grandson (Aethelstan) succeeded in driving the Vikings out from some parts of the Danelaw.

# Greenland

In around 980, a Norwegian Viking called Erik the Red left Norway for Iceland after being accused of several murders. Two years later Erik was once again on the run, after more killings.

## Ice and cliffs

Erik sailed west from Iceland. He decided to look for a land that had been sighted about sixty years before by a Viking called Gunnbjorn, who had been blown off course in a storm. The first glimpse of land was not encouraging – high cliffs and floating ice made landing impossible. But further round the coast, Erik found a landscape more like his Norwegian homeland. He spent three years exploring this new land before returning to Iceland. He deliberately gave it the name Greenland to encourage people to come and settle.

↑ This statue of Erik the Red stands in Narsarsuaq, Greenland, near the place where Erik once lived.

## Eastern and Western settlements

Even though the climate of Greenland was less cold then than it is now, it was still a hard place to live. Colonists from Iceland who followed Erik back to Greenland lived in two settlements on the southwest coast. These were the only places that had enough grazing land for all the cattle, horses, sheep, pigs and goats that the settlers brought with them. The two communities were called the Eastern and the Western settlements.

There were no trees to provide wood for buildings, so the settlers constructed their houses out of turf (grass) and stones. They relied on trade for essential items that were not available in Greenland, such as corn (which they could not grow). In return for these imported items they traded furs, sealskins, walrus tusks and teeth.

This chess piece is carved from walrus tusk. It was found on the Isle of Lewis in the Hebrides. ➡

# A new world

Some time around 985, a Viking called Bjarni Herjolfsson set sail from Iceland for Greenland. On the voyage he became lost in thick fog. When the fog cleared he glimpsed a low coastline with thick woods. He was possibly the first European to see North America.

## Vinland

Bjarni did not land on this strange coast but found his way back to Greenland, where he told tales of his sighting. A few years later, Leif Eriksson, son of Erik the Red, decided to try to find and explore this new land. He and his crew eventually landed in present-day Newfoundland, Canada, which Leif named Vinland ('Vine Land'). The name may have come from the large, red **huckleberries** that grew there, and which Leif may have mistaken for grapes.

This imaginative painting shows the Viking expedition landing on Vinland.

# Thorvald

Leif and his crew spent a winter in Vinland before returning to Greenland. His tales of the fertile soil, the endless woods and the mild climate encouraged his brother, Thorvald, to set sail for Vinland. But Thorvald was the first Viking to meet the local native Americans, who were not friendly towards the explorers. According to accounts in the **sagas**, Thorvald was killed by an arrow fired by one of the native Americans.

There were other Viking expeditions to Vinland, including an attempt to set up a **colony** there. But the Viking settlers soon found themselves in conflict with the native Americans. After three winters the colony was abandoned and the Vikings returned to Greenland.

## A Viking Object

This kind of pin was very popular in Norway, Ireland and Iceland. Pins and brooches were used by Viking men and women to fasten their clothing. Archaeological evidence such as this gives us vital clues about where the Vikings explored and settled.

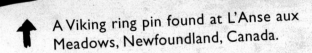

⬆ A Viking ring pin found at L'Anse aux Meadows, Newfoundland, Canada.

# The last attacks

In the 980s, after years of relative peace, a new wave of Viking attacks began on Britain. Once again, the Vikings wanted money and treasure.

## Danegeld

Viking raids along the British coastline in the 980s and 990s brought terror to the local people. In return for peace, the Vikings demanded payments in gold and silver, known as Danegeld. In 991, the Vikings defeated an English army at Maldon in Essex. The Vikings received a Danegeld payment of £10,000 in gold and silver from the English after this defeat.

## Danish rule

In 1013, the King of Denmark, Svein Forkbeard, arrived in England with a large army and was accepted as king of the Danelaw. The English king, Aethelred, was forced to flee to France.

⬆ A hoard of gold coins and jewellery found in Scandinavia. The Vikings collected vast amounts of treasure, some of which they buried for safekeeping.

Svein Forkbeard arrives in England with his Viking army.

Svein died in 1014, but his son Knut (Canute) became King of England after Aethelred's death in 1016. Knut ruled until his death in 1035, and was succeeded by his sons. In 1042, power passed back to the English once again when Aethelred's son, Edward (the Confessor), took the throne.

## King Knut
## Died 1035 CE

*Son of Svein Forkbeard, Knut invaded England in 1015 and fought many battles against Edmund Ironside (Aethelred's son). After Aethelred's death in 1016, Edmund and Knut agreed to divide England between them, but Edmund died soon after and Knut became king of all England. Knut was a good and successful ruler. He protected England against Viking raiders, and the country was peaceful and prosperous during his reign.*

# The end of the Viking Age

In 1066, the Norwegian king Harald Hardrada invaded Northumbria. He was defeated and killed at Stamford Bridge by the army of the English king, Harold, who had succeeded Edward earlier in the same year. Immediately after the victory at Stamford Bridge, Harold was forced to hurry south to meet another threat – an invasion by William of Normandy. Harold died at the Battle of Hastings, and England fell under Norman power. There were a few more Viking attacks, but by the 1080s the Viking Age had finally come to an end.

# Timeline

CE

| | |
|---|---|
| 789 | Vikings raid southern England |
| 793 | Vikings raid monastery of Lindisfarne, Northumbria |
| 794 | Viking raids on the monasteries of Jarrow and Wearmouth |
| 795 | Vikings raid monastery of St Columba on Iona |
| 800s | Vikings settle the Orkney and Shetland Islands |
| 815 | Floki of Rogaland sets out from the Faeroe Islands for Iceland |
| 830s | Viking attacks on western Europe and Ireland begin |
| 841 | Vikings establish a *longphort* at Dubh-Linn (Dublin) in Ireland |
| 843 | Vikings plunder Nantes, France |
| 844 | First recorded Viking raid in Spain |
| 845 | Ragnar Lodbrok leads a Viking army up the Seine to Paris |
| 865 | Arrival of a large Viking army in England |
| 869 | Vikings kill King Edmund in East Anglia |
| 870s | Start of mass Viking settlement of Iceland |
| c.880s | Treaty between kings Guthrum and Alfred creates the Danelaw |
| 885–6 | Viking siege of Paris |
| 911 | Normandy becomes a Viking territory under King Rollo |
| 930 | First meeting of the Althing – the Icelandic general assembly |
| c.982 | Erik the Red sails to Greenland. Start of Viking settlements in Greenland |
| c.985 | Bjarni Herjolfsson sights North America |
| 980s and 990s | New Viking attacks on England |
| c.1000 | Leif Eriksson sails to North America and names it Vinland |
| 1013 | Svein Forkbeard arrives in England and becomes king of the Danelaw |
| 1016 | Knut becomes King of England |
| 1066 | Norwegian king Harald Hadrada is defeated at the Battle of Stamford Bridge |
| 1080s | Final unsuccessful Viking attacks bring the Viking Age to a close |

# Glossary

**amber** fossilized tree resin – a hard, usually orange-coloured material that is prized for its colour and beauty

**archaeology** the study of ancient remains

**Byzantine Empire** the Eastern Roman Empire, centred on Constantinople, that survived until 1453

**chieftain** a leader

**colonize** to settle in a place

**colony** a place under the control of another country and settled by people from that country

**commerce** trade

**Danegeld** ransom paid to the Vikings, usually gold and silver coins

**Danelaw** the name for the area in England under Viking control from the 880s onwards

**famine** extreme lack of food

**glacier** a large mass of slow-moving ice

**heathen** a non-Christian (as referred to in writings by Christians)

**huckleberry** a large blueberry

**ingot** a block of metal

**iron ore** rock containing iron

**Islamic** describes people who are members of the Muslim faith

**livestock** animals such as cows, pigs or sheep

**longship** a Viking warship

**monastery** a place where monks live and worship

**Norsemen** Vikings from Scandinavia

**Old Norse** the language spoken by Scandinavians during the Viking Age

**pagan** someone who holds religious beliefs that vary from the main world religions

**plague** a disease that spreads and kills many people if untreated

**plunder** to steal goods forcibly

**raider** someone who makes a surprise attack and takes loot

**ransom** money that is demanded in return for something

**saga** a long tale of heroic achievements, usually in Old Norse or Old Icelandic

**shrine** a place that is regarded as holy

**siege** a military operation during which forces surround a city or fort and cut off the people inside from all supplies and help

**treaty** a formal agreement

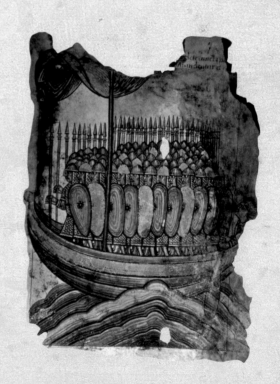

# Index

# Resources

*History from Objects: The Vikings*, Colin Malam, Wayland 2010

*All about Ancient Peoples: The Vikings*, Anita Ganeri, Watts, 2009

*Men, Women and Children in Viking Times*, Colin Hynson, Wayland, 2009

*http://www.jorvik-viking-centre.co.uk/*
Website of the Jorvik Viking Centre in York.

*http://www.bbc.co.uk/schools/primaryhistory/vikings/*
BBC site for children about the Vikings.